Shine Your Light
Devotional

_____

Given to

_____

By

_____

On this date

Published in Nashville, Tennessee, by Tommy Nelson. Tommy Nelson is a registered trademark of Thomas Nelson, Inc.

Published in association with the literary agency of Alive Communications, Inc., 7680 Goddard Street, Suite 200, Colorado Springs, CO 80920. www.alivecommunications.com

Thomas Nelson, Inc., titles may be purchased in bulk for educational, business, fund-raising, or sales promotional use. For information, please e-mail SpecialMarkets@ThomasNelson.com.

Unless otherwise noted, Scripture quotations are from the International Children's Bible®. © 1986, 1988, 1999 by Thomas Nelson, Inc. All rights reserved. Scriptures marked NLT are from Holy Bible, New Living Translation. © 1996. Used by permission of Tyndale House Publishers, Inc., Wheaton, Illinois 60189. All rights reserved.

ISBN-13: 978-1-4003-2069-1

Library of Congress Cataloging-in-Publication Data
Walsh, Sheila, 1956-
  Shine your light devotional / by Sheila Walsh ; illustrations by Natasha Kuricheva.
      pages cm. -- (God's little angel)
  ISBN 978-1-4003-2069-1 (hardcover)
1. Girls--Prayers and devotions. 2. Christian education--Activity programs. I. Kuricheva, Natasha, illustrator. II. Title.

BV4860.W357 2012
242'.62--dc23
                                2012031016

17 18 19 20 DBS 6 5 4 3 2
www.thomasnelson.com

Shine Your Light
Devotional

Sheila Walsh

With Jean Fischer

A Division of Thomas Nelson Publishers

NASHVILLE   DALLAS   MEXICO CITY   RIO DE JANEIRO

Contents

Introduction

Hello, little lightning bug! You probably haven't been called that before, but do you know that when you love God, your life becomes a light that shines for Him? He loves you so much and uses lots of ways to show His love. He gave the Bible to guide you, He gave you parents to take care of you, and He even sent angels to watch over you. But did you know that He wants to use you to show God's love too? Matthew 5:16 says:

"You should be a light for other people. Live so that they will see the good things you do. Live so that they will praise your Father in heaven."

So you see, you are one of God's bright lights! These devotions will show you how to let that light shine each day—by doing things such as thanking God, learning His Word, telling others about Him, and showing His love to everyone you meet. And lots of fun features will focus on ways to keep that light growing:

- ❀ *Bright Ideas*—*Cool things to say and do.*
- ❀ *Dear God and Dear Jesus*—*Simple prayers to get you connected.*
- ❀ *In the Spotlight*—*New words to learn.*
- ❀ *Sparkling Scriptures*—*Memory verses.*
- ❀ *If You Were There*—*Ways to imagine yourself in the story.*
- ❀ *Searchlights*—*Hidden treasure for you to find.*
- ❀ *Shine Your Light*—*Ideas for letting God's light shine in your life every day.*

So let's get busy, serve God and others with a grateful heart, and let our lights shine. Your one life can make such a difference in this world—so shine on!

You Are God's Special Creation

Do you know how special you are? There is no one in the whole world exactly like you. You are one of a kind, wonderful, and amazing. Even better, you are a precious child of God.

God's book, the Bible, can help you learn about God and yourself. It says that God made you. He knew you even before you were formed inside of your mom's body, and He made you exactly the way that He wanted. God chose the colors of your eyes, hair, and skin. He chose your parents, grandparents, sisters, and brothers. He knows your family and friends because He made them too. God already knows everything that will happen in your life, the special skills and talents you have, the kind of work you will do when you grow up, and the person you might marry someday. Nothing about you is a secret to God. When He looks at you, He sees somebody awesome. He promises to be with you each and every day, and God will never, ever stop loving you.

The next time you look in the mirror, think about how wonderful you are. Then say a little prayer to God, and thank Him for making YOU!

Sparkling SCRIPTURE

"You made my whole being. You formed me in my mother's body. I praise you because you made me in an amazing and wonderful way. What you have done is wonderful. I know this very well."

PSALM 139:13–14

Ask an adult to help you make a mirror.
You will need:

- *A piece of white cardboard 12 inches square*
- *A piece of aluminum foil 11 inches square*
- *Paste*
- *Crayons*

Bright IDEA

Paste the dull side of the foil onto the cardboard, leaving a white border all around. Smooth out the wrinkles. If you want, write *Look Who God Made* or *God Says I'm Beautiful* on the border, and decorate the border with your crayons. Now look in your mirror and see the special person God made! Isn't she lovely?

Dear God

Thank You for making me and for making me special. I love You so much! Amen.

Shine your LIGHT

Think of several reasons why your parents and family are extra special. Does your dad ride bikes with you? Does your papa cheer when you score a goal? Is your mom the best cookie decorator in the world? Draw a picture that shows your family why they are special. If you want, write You Are Special on the picture.

Only One God

*G*od made you in His image. That means He made you to be like Him. God made you to be loving, good, kind, fair, honest, and caring. But just like you are a one-of-a-kind person, God is a one-of-a-kind God. He didn't make you like Him in every way. God is perfect, and no one can or ever will be as perfect as He is. He can do many things that you can't.

The God of the Bible is the one and only God. He is perfectly good and kind and also very strong and powerful. There is nothing that He can't do. He has the amazing power to see and hear everything and be everywhere all at the same time. He knows everything that happens, and He knows about it before it happens. God is the great King of everything. He is in charge of heaven and earth, the sky and stars, you, me, animals, angels, everything.

Words can't describe how much God loves you and how much He wants you to love Him back. There are many ways to do that. You can tell God you love Him in your prayers, sing songs to Him, read the Bible, and tell others about how wonderful He is. Can you think of other ways to show Him your love?

Search LIGHT Read the devotional again to find the answer to this question: *What are some things God can do that you can't do?*

Shine your LIGHT

God loves it when a family prays together. Thanking God aloud in prayer is one way to speak about His one-and-only greatness. Get your family together, and teach them to say this prayer: "We thank You, God, for the world so sweet. We thank You, God, for the food we eat. We thank You, God, for the birds that sing. We thank You, God, for everything." Get in the habit of praying together every morning or every night at bedtime.

With All My Heart

How big is your heart? Make a tight fist. It's about that big. But the word *heart* means more than the organ in your body. It also means the center of who you are, your deepest thoughts and feelings.

The Bible says you should love God with all of your heart. In other words, you should give God your very best love all the time. Think about who or what you love the most. God wants you to love Him even more. You can give God your best love not only by worshipping Him but also by loving others the way He does. God always loves people no matter what they say or do. He may hate how they behave, but He loves them, and that is how He wants you to love.

How much love do you think your heart can hold? God made your heart so special that it can hold all the love you can imagine and more, and God wants to fill it up. Ask Him today to fill up your heart with His love.

Sparkling **SCRIPTURE**

"Love the Lord your God with all your heart, soul and strength."

DEUTERONOMY 6:5

Draw a big heart. Inside of it, print the words *God's Love.* That's where God's love is, inside your heart!

Bright IDEA

Dear God

Thank You for filling up my heart with Your love. I love You too! Teach me to share Your love with everyone I meet. Amen.

Shine your LIGHT

Did you know that your heart can never be too full of love? There is enough room in your heart for all the love you can imagine! This week, see if you can find a new person to love. Make a new friend, and show him or her God's love by being kind. By the end of the week, you'll find that your heart has grown even bigger!

The Best Gift Ever!

The world was messed up with sin. People did bad things that upset God and made Him sad. No matter how hard they tried, people just couldn't stay away from sin, so God made a plan to help them.

God loved the people of the world so much that He decided to give them a very special gift—His Son, Jesus. God sent Jesus into the world as a baby. When Jesus grew up, He taught the people about God, and He did amazing miracles. Before long, thousands of people followed Him to see what He would say and do, and many believed in Him.

But not everyone was happy with Jesus. Some did not believe that He was the Son of God. They worried that He was becoming too popular. They wanted to kill Him, and that's just what they did. They killed Jesus by nailing His hands and feet to a big, wooden cross.

Jesus could have asked God to save Him, but He didn't. Jesus wanted all of us to live with Him and God in heaven someday, and He knew that sin had no place in heaven. So He agreed to die as punishment for our sins—all the bad things we would ever do. If we believe that Jesus took the punishment for us and we follow Him, then we can go to heaven one day and live forever with Jesus, God's best gift to us. He is our only way to heaven.

You might feel sad that Jesus died, but there is a happy ending. Jesus didn't stay dead for long. God brought Him back to life so people could see that He really is the Son of God. Then Jesus went up into heaven to make a special place for us to live someday.

Think about how Jesus died on the cross so God could forgive your sin. Wasn't that an amazing act of love?

In the **Spotlight**

Sin: the many ways that people disobey God

Sparkling **SCRIPTURE**

"For God loved the world so much that he gave his only Son. God gave his Son so that whoever believes in him may not be lost, but have eternal life."

John 3:16

Bright IDEA

You will need at least 20 blank note cards. On all but one card, paste or draw a picture of an animal (dog, cat, wolf, lion). On the remaining card, paste or draw a picture of the earth. Shuffle the cards picture-side down and put them in a stack. Take turns with a friend drawing a card from the top of the stack. Don't let your friend see what it is. If you draw an animal card, act it out. If your friend can guess the animal, he or she earns 2 points. If you draw the earth card, you must recite John 3:16, and you earn 5 points. Keep playing until one player earns 25 points.

Shine your LIGHT

Ask a parent to help you find John 3:16 in your Bible. (Hint: It's in the New Testament.) Then share the message with your friends. Tell them that God sent Jesus to the world to save us all from our sins. Good news like that is easy to share!

Jesus—The Light of the World

Can you imagine a world without light? People would be bumping into each other everywhere and stumbling over anything that got in their way. Everyone would feel grumpy living in the darkness. Sound crazy? Even before He made people, God knew that they would need light. He didn't want His people tripping and falling all the time, and He knew we would need light to live. So, on the very first day, God made light, and He said, "Light is good!"

God sent another kind of Light into the world—Jesus. When people don't know God, it is like they live in darkness. Jesus came to fix that. He said, "I am the Light of the World." He came to save people from the darkness of living in sin apart from God. When people believe in and love God, then their world feels brighter.

Do you love God? His light can shine through you, and you can bring more light into the world by telling your friends all about Him.

In the Spotlight

Darkness and Light: The Bible calls sin "darkness." When you live with sin, it is like stumbling and bumping around in a dark forest. You can't see right from wrong or find your way. Jesus said that He is the Light of the World because His love for you shines big and bright. Jesus is like a light that helps you to see right from wrong. His light shows us the way out of darkness and toward Him and heaven instead.

Bright IDEA

Turn on a flashlight. Shine its light up close on different objects. Try a book, a piece of paper, your hand, a towel, and a rock. Do you see how the light shines through some objects and not others? When you believe in and love God, His light shines through you like a warm, bright light shining into your heart!

Dear *Jesus*

Thank You for being the Light of my world. I want to be a light for You too. Help me bring God's love into the world, and teach me to brighten the lives of others by telling them all about You. Amen.

Shine your LIGHT

Think about one or two people you know who might need some of God's light. Maybe they are sad, sick, or lonely. Give them a few rays of God's light this week—share a Bible verse, tell them a great story, or give them a flower to brighten their day.

Just Like Jesus

You are watching a video with your little brother. Suddenly he gets up, takes out the DVD, and puts one in that he wants to watch. He does that a lot lately because he just learned how to use the DVD player. What should you do? You could get mad and yell at him. You could put the DVD you want to watch back in the player and give his DVD to the dog as a Frisbee. Or you could gently remind your little brother about sharing. That's showing patience and kindness—just like Jesus would!

Jesus tried to make the world a better place wherever He went. He always acted in ways that were kind, gentle, loving, helpful, and forgiving. And when He saw people doing wrong, He taught them to do what is right. Everything Jesus did pleased His Father, God.

You are God's child too, and He wants to be pleased with everything you say and do. God is happy when you act like Jesus. Being like Him will make your light shine brightly wherever you go. How much do you know about Jesus? What words can you think of to describe Him? The more you learn about Jesus, the easier it is to become more like Him.

Have a patience contest with a family member. For a whole day, keep track of times when you are patient (write them down so you won't forget). At the end of the day, the two of you can share your lists and see whose list is longer. But remember, God loves you both the same!

Search LIGHT

Be on the lookout today for people who act in helpful ways like Jesus would. Can you find three people acting helpful? How about five?

Shine your LIGHT

During the next few days, look for ways to be kind like Jesus. One simple way to be kind is to smile. How many different people can you smile at? Your teacher? The lady at the grocery store? What about the boy next door, even on days when he is grumpy? Let others see Jesus in you!

The Bible Is Our Lamp

Have you been overnight camping or had a sleepover outside in a tent? Was it really dark but really fun? Maybe you had a campfire, flashlight, or lantern to help you make the dark seem more like daytime and to light your way as you walked through the dark.

The Bible is like a flashlight or lantern that shines in a dark place and makes it brighter. It uses God's own words to brighten your way through life and lead you in the right direction. The Bible teaches you right from wrong and shows you how to act around others. Best of all, it tells you about Jesus and helps you understand God better and how very much He loves you.

The Bible has many words, and God doesn't expect you to know all of them by heart. But when you hear a special verse that makes you feel closer to God, memorize it. The more of

His words you store in your heart, the brighter your life will be because you will be filling it with His light!

 *Thank You for the Bible. Whenever I read it I feel closer to You. It's like You have written those words just for me! Amen.*

Sparkling SCRIPTURE

"Your word is like a lamp for my feet and a light for my way."

PSALM 119:105

Can you find Psalm 119:105 in your Bible? Hints: The book of Psalms is very near the middle of most Bibles. You will find it in the Old Testament between the books of Job and Proverbs.

Shine your LIGHT

Make bookmarks for your friends. Ask an adult to help you cut thick paper into 3-by-6-inch rectangles. Write Psalm 119:105 on each one, and decorate them any way you want. When your friends use their bookmarks, they will be reminded of God's light!

What Should I Do?

*P*retend that you and your best friend are playing checkers. It's your move, and then you see it—you're stuck. You have three checkers left, and it seems like whichever one you move, she will be able to jump you. Maybe there's a way out. You wish you knew more about playing checkers. Then you would have a better chance of staying in the game. Finally, you move a checker, and your friend jumps you—not once or twice, but three times! All your checkers are gone, and she wins the game. How are you going to act when you lose?

God gave us the Bible for learning how to get out of sticky situations. The Bible is useful for showing people what is wrong in their lives and teaching them how to get along and learn to live right. The Bible won't tell you how to win a game of checkers, but it will show you how to be an honest player and a good loser. It will teach you to get along with your friends without arguing or getting mad. The Bible says to try to get along with people all the time as best as you can.

So what *would* you do when your friend wins the game? Would you tell her, "Good job," or would you get mad and refuse to play with her anymore? Knowing what God says in the Bible can help you decide.

Sparkling SCRIPTURE

"All Scripture is given by God and is useful for teaching and showing people what is wrong in their lives. It is useful for correcting faults and teaching how to live right."

2 Timothy 3:16

Each question below has a
Bible verse that holds one
of God's answers. Ask a
parent to read these answers
for you.

- *What should I do when I feel angry? Proverbs 15:18*
- *What should I do when someone is mean to me? 1 Peter 3:9*
- *What should I do when I don't know what to do? Luke 6:31*

*I want to learn all about You.
Please help me understand Your words
in the Bible and behave the way You
want me to. Amen.*

Shine your LIGHT

God's answers for life's problems are in the Bible, but if you don't read it to find out what's inside, you won't know what God wants you to do. Ask your mom or dad to help you memorize one or two Bible verses every week. The more you know about God, the easier it will become to know what to do.

Let It Shine!

*J*esus often told little stories. Some were like riddles because they made people think. In one of His stories, He said, "No one takes a light and puts it under a bowl or hides it. Instead, he puts the light on a lampstand so that the people who come in can see" (Luke 11:33).

What do you think Jesus' story about the lampstand means? It would be crazy to take something as wonderful and necessary as light and hide it under a bowl where no one could see it. It would be just as crazy to hide God and all of His goodness. God wants everyone in the whole world to know Him. When you obey Him and share Him and the wonderful things He says and does, it is like putting a lamp on a stand where it lights up a room.

Telling your friends about God and showing His love by setting a good example shines God's light on them. God brightens a person's life, just like a light on a stand brightens a room. Ask Him to help you live the way He wants you to live. Then His love will shine through you like a very bright light!

In the **Spotlight**

Lampstand: a place to put a lamp so it lights up the room

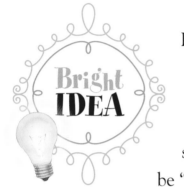

Bright IDEA

Play a game of shadow tag with your friends. Go outside on a sunny afternoon and have everyone find their own shadow. Choose one friend to be "it." Everyone runs around, and "it" tries to tag people by making her shadow touch theirs. When a player's shadow is tagged, that person becomes "it." The game goes on until everyone's shadow has been tagged at least once.

Do you think you could play this game outside in the dark? Why or why not? Living without God's love in your heart is like a day without sunshine!

Sparkling **SCRIPTURE**

"You should be a light for other people. Live so that they will see the good things you do. Live so that they will praise your Father in heaven."

MATTHEW 5:16

Shine your LIGHT

Missionaries help shine God's light on the world by teaching people near and far about Jesus. Check with your pastor and see what you can do to help a missionary in another part of the world. Maybe you can donate some money from your allowance. Or you can help your family send a care package—be sure to include one of the bookmarks you made with a special Bible verse on it.

Stir It Up!

When you make a cake, you put all the ingredients in a bowl and stir them up. Without stirring and making the ingredients work together, you would have just a box of cake mix, some eggs, and water.

God likes to stir things up too. He wants to bring His people together to serve others. Jesus set a good example. When Jesus saw a need, He found a way to fill it. He was the leader, but He didn't work alone. He got people together to spread the Word about God's love. He sent His helpers, called "disciples," into the world. They got people together, sort of like mixing ingredients. They stirred up other people's love for God and got them to share it.

God's helpers share His love in big and small ways. Some travel around the world to help people and tell them about Jesus. Others stay in their own towns and help out there. You can share God's love by helping whenever you can. You will like the way you feel when you help others and stir up their love for God. It will make you want to help even more.

Bright IDEA

If your church sponsors missionaries working in another country, see if you can find out where the missionaries are by looking at a map. Does your church have an address for the missionaries? You can draw them a picture or write them a letter to say that you are praying for them.

Search LIGHT

Jesus chose twelve men to help Him spread God's Word and stir up God's love. See if you can find their names in the Bible using these clues:

* Start at the first book of the New Testament.
* The chapter number rhymes with "men," and it's not "hen"!
* Jesus' helpers were sometimes called "apostles."

Did you find them?

Bless Your helpers wherever they go, and keep them safe as they spread Your love. Amen.

Shine your LIGHT

Ask your parents to call a family meeting to talk about ways you can work together to spread God's love in your town. Make a list of ideas. Stir things up! Get your family excited about working with God.

A Golden Rule That Shines

Sometimes people we know are grumpy, selfish, or unkind. It's no fun to be around them. They make you feel sad and maybe angry. They can be hard to love. But guess what? God wants you to love those people. That doesn't mean you like what they do. It means that you love them anyway, just the way they are, the same way that God loves you.

Jesus said that you should behave toward others exactly the way that you want them to behave toward you. His rule has a special name. It is called the Golden Rule, and it is very important. Think about how you would want someone to treat you if you were grumpy, selfish, or unkind. Then act that way! Let your light be golden and bright. In every

47

situation, you should try to love people the same way that God loves you—with kindness, understanding, and forgiveness.

Sparkling SCRIPTURE

"Do for other people the same things you want them to do for you."

Matthew 7:12

Make a "Do for Others" necklace.

You will need:

* *A piece of colored yarn about 14 inches long*
* *3 three-inch circles cut from white cardboard or heavy paper*
* *Crayons*
* *Elbow macaroni or beads, if you want to add them to your necklace*

Print the word *Do* on one circle, *for* on the second, and *Others* on the third. Decorate the circles with your crayons. Ask a parent to punch two holes near the top of the circles so you can string them onto the yarn. If you want, you can string beads or elbow macaroni to decorate your necklace. Now, tie the yarn around your neck and wear your necklace to remind your friends to do for others. Or you could make necklaces for them!

Dear Jesus

Help me
be kind and
loving to
everyone,
even the
people who
aren't kind
and loving
toward me.
Amen.

Shine your LIGHT

People who are hard to love might need some forgiving and kind words. When you don't know how to love someone, ask God to help you. He is always there, ready to guide you to do what is right. Try doing something kind this week for one person who is hard to love.

Putting Jesus First

LUKE 10:38–42

Mary and Martha were sisters and Jesus' friends. One day Jesus stopped at Martha's house to visit, and Mary was there too. Both sisters felt happy about Jesus' visit, but Martha worried because her house wasn't neat and clean. She wanted everything perfect for Jesus. So Martha got busy. She went to work fixing food and cleaning her house. Meanwhile, Mary sat at Jesus' feet, listening to all the wonderful things He said. She loved hearing Him teach about God, and she didn't want to miss a single word.

When Martha saw Mary sitting there, she felt angry. *Mary should be helping me,* she thought, *but instead she's sitting with Jesus*

WELCOME

while I do all the work. So Martha walked right up to Jesus and said, "Jesus, don't you care that my sister has left me to do all the work? Tell her to help me!"

Jesus answered, "Martha, Martha, you are getting worried and upset about too many things. Only one thing is important. Mary has chosen the right thing, and it will never be taken away from her."

What do you think Jesus meant? He was telling Martha that He was way more important than the work she had to do. In fact, putting Him first is the most important thing of all. Jesus wants to come first in everything you think, say, and do too.

Does Jesus come first in your life?

If *you* were there...

Imagine that you are Martha in the story. How would you feel if Jesus made a surprise visit to your house? Would you worry that your room wasn't clean enough for Him to see or that you hadn't made something special for Him to eat?

True or False? Mary and Martha were best friends. You'll find the answer in the story.

Bright IDEA

Play this Mary and Martha follow-the-leader game with your friends. The leader does four actions in a row very quickly (flap arms, pat head, touch nose, touch toes). The other players must do exactly what the leader did or they are "Marthas" and are out of the game. Keep playing until there is only one player left. That player is "Mary."

Remember: Jesus is our leader, and it is important to put Him first and pay close attention to everything He says.

Shine your LIGHT

Why is Jesus so special that He deserves all of your attention? Because Jesus is God's Son, and everything He says and does is perfect, good, true, and wise. If you make other things more important than Jesus, you might not have any time left for Him. This week set aside a special time each day to spend with Jesus. You can talk with Him in prayer, read about Him in the Bible, or sing songs that talk about His love.

Love Is . . .

I love you!" I hope you say those words often to your family and especially to God. They may seem like little words, but they have loads of power. Love is more than a feeling in your heart. Love is showing patience and kindness. It is giving up a part of yourself to help others and put them first.

You show love by being nice to people instead of being selfish or rude. Real love, the kind the Bible tells about, means looking for the good in people. If you hate, argue, or fight, you aren't showing God's love. His love is always good. It is forgiving, and it lasts forever.

It's hard to love all the time. People mess up. God is the only One whose love is perfect. But He wants you to try your best to show your best love to everyone. Along with saying, "I love you," practice showing love in whatever you do. The more love you show, the more it will reflect back to you like a light shining on a mirror.

Sparkling SCRIPTURE

"Love is patient and kind. Love is not jealous,
it does not brag, and it is not proud."

1 CORINTHIANS 13:4

Bright IDEA

Make a "love collage" using photos and pictures you draw or cut from old magazines. Use pictures of things you love to see, eat, and do. Add pictures of the people you love, including you! Here are some words you could add to your collage: Love is . . .

- Patient
- Kind
- Truthful
- Hopeful
- Forgiving

- Everything good
- Not jealous
- Not rude
- Not selfish
- God

Shine your LIGHT

Choose one person in your family today, and try to show him or her your best love all day long. Instead of saying, "I love you," show it in everything you do. At the end of the day, share with that person what you have learned about love.

Take a Bow!

*I*magine you are asked to sing a solo in church next Sunday. You are excited but a little scared. Everyone says you sing really well, but there's a small voice inside you that whispers, *What if I forget the words? What if I sing out of tune? What if people laugh at me?* Sometimes things feel scary because you don't know what to expect. But when that voice says, "You can't," your answer should be, "Yes, I can!"

God puts special gifts into all His children. Maybe you sing, dance, draw, or something else. Whatever your gifts are, God wants you to share them. He put trust inside of you as a way to help you be brave. Trusting in Jesus pushes those *I can't* thoughts right out of your head because trusting in Him makes you strong.

What are you good at doing? God wants you to share it.

If you feel uncomfortable sharing your gifts, then call on Jesus. He is fearless and brave, and He will help you. Jesus doesn't ask us to be perfect, just to be willing.

In the **Spotlight**

"Christ" is another name for Jesus. Trusting in Christ helps you be strong and brave.

Sparkling **SCRIPTURE**

"I can do all things through Christ because he gives me strength."

PHILIPPIANS 4:13

Search LIGHT

Finish this sentence: Trusting in Jesus makes you _____. You will find the answer in today's devotion.

Make up a song called "Yes, I Can!" Make it a song about Jesus. After you've practiced your song and know it by heart, sing it

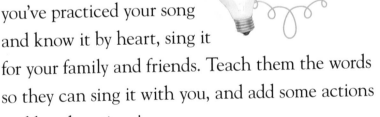

Bright IDEA

for your family and friends. Teach them the words so they can sing it with you, and add some actions and hand motions!

Shine your LIGHT

Memorize this little prayer so it will be with you whenever you need it: "Jesus, whenever I say, 'I can't,' remind me that I can. Amen." Teach the prayer to your friends so they can say it too—whenever and wherever they are!

Jesus Loves You

MARK 10:13–16

*J*esus was so popular that wherever He went crowds waited to meet Him. Moms and dads brought their children to Jesus just so He could pray for them.

One day a group of little children stood all around Jesus. The special helpers, Jesus' disciples, decided that the children might be bothering Jesus, so they told them to go away.

But Jesus said, "Stop! Let the little children come to me." He took the children into His arms and blessed them. He even told the grown-ups that it was important for them to believe and trust in Him just the way the children did.

Jesus loves kids. He is never, ever too busy for children. He promises to love you and be there for you all day, every day, and through every night. And when Jesus makes a promise, He keeps it! You can't see Him, but you can feel Jesus in your heart. You can always depend on Him to love and take care of you.

Sparkling SCRIPTURE

"All your children will be taught by the Lord, and they will have much peace."

Isaiah 54:13

If *you* were there...

Imagine you were one of the kids visiting with Jesus that day. What would you have said to Him?

Bright IDEA

Play hide-and-seek with a group of your friends. When the person who is "it" finds a hider, that hider joins "it" in the search. Before long, you will have most of your friends searching with you for the last hidden person.

If you hide really well, it may take your friends a long time to find you, right? But Jesus knows where you are all the time, and you can never hide from Him. Jesus loves you so much that He will never, ever leave you. Remind your friends of that when you're playing hide-and-seek with them.

I love You, Jesus. Thank You for always loving me and living in my heart. Amen.

Shine your LIGHT

Ask your pastor or Bible class teacher for the names of people from your church who are sick and unable to come to services. Make each person a card that says, "Jesus loves you!" It will be a daily reminder of Jesus' love.

Turn on Your Willpower

Come on. Everyone else is doing it!" Has a friend said that to you? Did you think, *This is not a good idea?* Even when you know something is wrong, it's hard not to go along with your friends. That's when you need to turn on your willpower.

When you know you shouldn't do something, you can trust God to help you stay away from it. The better you know Him and what He says in the Bible, the easier it is to know and do what is right. What would you do if a friend asked you to go swimming when no grown-ups were around, or if you and he wanted a brownie, but your mom told you not to eat one before supper? God gives you strength to stand up to what you know is wrong. All you need to do is ask Him to help you make wise choices.

If you practice willpower, you will get really good at it. Start working on your willpower today. Pray that God will make you strong in the places you feel weak.

In the Spotlight

Willpower: learning to control how you behave

Ask a family member to join you in a willpower practice challenge. Get a treat that you both really, really like to eat, and put it where you can see it. Can you both go all day without eating it? Try it with your dog too—that can be tricky!

Shine your LIGHT

Having willpower keeps you from doing dangerous things like running out in the street toward the ice-cream truck. But willpower is something you have to learn. If you have very young brothers, sisters, or friends, help them learn to have willpower and to make wise choices about the things they do. Ask God to help you be a good teacher as He watches over all of you.

Hi, God. It's Me!

Prayer is talking to God like He's your best friend forever—because He is! He loves you, and He always listens to your prayers. God wants you to tell Him about your problems, things you don't understand, your secrets and joys, and your needs. He wants you to ask Him for things that will make you a better person, and He wants you to pray for others.

When you pray for others, there is a long list of people to choose from. Of course, you pray for your family and friends, but you can also pray for your teachers, for the missionaries who teach others about Jesus, and for the leaders of your church, city, state, and country. Sick people need prayers, and so do those who are sad and lonely. People who don't know Jesus need prayers too. You should pray that they get to know Jesus like you do.

Prayer is much more than talking to God. It is one way to feel close to God and show Him how very much you love Him.

Search **LIGHT** Be on the lookout for people who might need a prayer. Do you see someone who looks sad? Say a prayer for him. How about someone behaving badly? Pray for her too. Sometimes God will put a thought in your head to pray for someone you see. If that happens, even if you don't know the person, say a silent prayer and ask God to help her.

In the **Spotlight**

Silent prayer is thinking your prayers instead of saying them out loud. God hears your prayers whether you think them or say them!

Bright **IDEA**

Go on some silent-prayer walks with your family. Walk through your neighborhood, and say a silent prayer for the people who live in each house along the way. Go to the zoo and pray for the animals, or go to the park and pray for the other kids there. Where else could you go on your silent-prayer walks?

Shine your LIGHT

Set aside one day each week to pray for a certain group of people. Making a list or writing it on a calendar will help you remember. On Monday, you might pray for your teachers, on Tuesday for people who are sick, on Wednesday for missionaries, on Thursday for our president and those who lead our nation. Pray together as a family, and suggest people you know who need some prayers.

Say It Loud, Say It Strong

MATTHEW 21:12–16

Jesus went into the temple one day—a temple is like a church—and He saw people selling stuff. It looked like one big garage sale! That made Jesus angry. A temple is a place to worship God, not a place to buy and sell. So Jesus told the people to get out of there. Some children were nearby, and when they saw all the good things Jesus did, they started yelling, really loudly, "Hosanna to the Son of David!" That was like saying Jesus was the next king. When the temple leaders heard the children shouting praises to Jesus like He was their king, they told the children to be quiet. "Do you hear what they're saying?" they asked Jesus.

Jesus answered with a verse from the Bible. He said, "You have taught children and babies to sing praises" (Matthew 21:16). It meant that from the time you are little all the way to the end of your life, you should never be shy about praising God.

Jesus was never shy about sharing the Good News—the Bible—with others. He wanted everyone to believe in God.

How about you? Are you shy when it comes to telling others about Jesus? Don't be. Sharing your love for Him is the best thing you can do.

If *you* were there...

What would it have been like to be one of the children in the temple with Jesus that day? Would you have been nervous? Would you have used your strongest voice to praise Him? Praising Jesus is always a good thing to do!

Bright IDEA

A Good News scavenger hunt is lots of fun, especially when you're in a car or while you're waiting at a restaurant, but you can play almost anywhere. Look for something that begins with each of these letters: G, O, O, D, N, E, W, and S. The first one to find something for all the letters and call out "Good News" wins.

G = *grass, garage, grapes*

O = *olives, orange car*

O = *owl, orange sign*

D = *dog, drink*

N = *nachos, nine, nest*

E = *eggs, eight, elevator*

W = *woman, wheel, window*

S = *sidewalk, stop sign, sandwich*

Sparkling SCRIPTURE

"I am not ashamed of the Good News. It is the power God uses to save everyone who believes."

Romans 1:16

Shine your LIGHT

Have you ever watched fireflies on a summer night? Everywhere they go, they flash their lights in bright little bursts. Sharing the Good News is a lot like that. Wherever you go, you can let your light shine by sharing little bits of Scripture with your friends. Share the Good News this week. Tell your friends about Bible verses that help you stay close to Jesus.

God Is Great, and We Are Grateful

*I*magine helping someone day after day and never hearing a "thank you." Wouldn't it hurt your feelings to think that you weren't appreciated? God must feel that way sometimes too. He never takes a break from caring for, helping, and giving us what we need, but so often we forget to thank Him.

Did you have fun playing with your friends today? Do you have food to eat and a safe place to live? Have you noticed all the great, bright, and wonderful things in God's creation: birds singing, flowers blooming, stars twinkling like a million fireflies way up in the sky? Say, "Thank You, God! Thank You, thank You, thank You!"

God wants us to be grateful to Him for everything, all the time, no matter what, and He wants us to be grateful to others too. Try it out. Go to your mom and dad today and tell them, "Thank you for everything you do for me." See if it makes them smile.

In the **Spotlight**

Grateful: another word for "thankful"

Take turns with a friend telling each other one thing that you are grateful for. Can you each come up with a list of ten? How about twenty? When you finish, say a little prayer to thank God for the things on your lists.

Bright IDEA

Shine your LIGHT

Do you have toys that you don't play with anymore? You could donate your gently used toys to kids who don't have as much as you do. You can be grateful that you have enough toys that you can give some away, and they will be grateful for getting them!

Sparkling Promises

How often do you make promises? Do you always keep them? When someone promises you something and then doesn't do it, how does it make you feel? Broken promises can be hurtful and disappointing. People mess up sometimes and don't always keep their word, but there is Someone who never, ever breaks a promise—God!

When our great and mighty God says something, He doesn't change His mind about it. The Bible is filled with His wonderful promises, and when God makes a promise, you can always count on Him to do what He says.

God wants your promises to sparkle, like His, with truthfulness. He wants you to be just like Him and keep the promises you make to others.

When you keep your word, people will know they can trust you the same way that they can trust God.

Sparkling **SCRIPTURE**

"The Lord will keep his promises. With love he takes care of all he has made."

Psalm 145:13

Who never, ever breaks a promise? If you aren't sure, go back and read the devotion again.

Shine your LIGHT

Try this activity with your family. Have everyone write on a piece of paper something they need help with this week. Fold the papers in half, and then put them in a bowl. Each family member picks out a paper and promises to help with that need. We should all work hard to keep our promises the same way God keeps His.

Look at What God Did!

Do you enjoy looking at the stars? Even beyond the ones you can see, there are millions and millions more, and God made them all! He made everything in the sky and on the earth. If you could walk all the way around Earth, you would see hundreds of interesting plants, insects, and animals. You would travel across tall hills and mountains, deep valleys, streams, oceans, and deserts. You might even pass a few volcanoes on the way. God made those too. He made the wind and the rain, snow and ice, rainbows, and seasons that change. In fact, you can think of the earth and sky like a big painting that God hasn't finished yet. There is no end to His creations.

When we look at God's creations, we think, *Wow! Isn't that amazing?* And we thank Him because everything He gives us is good and wonderful and shows how much He loves us.

Look out your window. What good things do you see? Bow your head and say, "Thank You, God!"

Sparkling SCRIPTURE

"You are the only Lord. You made the heavens, even the highest heavens. You made all the stars. You made the earth and everything that is on it. You made the seas and everything that is in them. You give life to everything. The heavenly army worships you."

Nehemiah 9:6

What is your favorite thing God created? Draw a picture of it. Then tell someone why you think it is God's best creation.

Bright IDEA

Dear God

Thank You for all the wonderful things You have made. Help me respect and care for Your earth, its people, and the animals. Amen.

Shine your LIGHT

You can help keep God's creation neat and clean by recycling and picking up any litter you see. Some communities have special days when citizens help with cleaning parks, beaches, and other areas. Find out what you and your family can do to help.

Let's Be Friends

"That's mine!"

"No, it's mine!"

"I saw it first."

"No, *I* did!"

Friends fuss with each other sometimes, even the very best of friends. It's not easy to always get along, but that's what God would like you to do. It makes Him happy when, instead of fighting, His kids work things out. When you are kind to one another, you are sharing God's love and being a good servant to Him. The Bible tells us what it takes to be a good servant: "A servant of the Lord must not quarrel! He must be kind to everyone. . . . He must be patient" (2 Timothy 2:24).

You can get along better with your friends by sharing the things God has blessed you with, like your toys. If a friend says mean things to you, answer with kind words. When you disagree, talk about the problem. If you can't settle it on your own, ask a grown-up for help, and accept what he or she says without getting angry.

The next time you and a friend start quarreling, stop. Think about what God wants you to do. Then say, "Let's be friends."

Dear God

Help me to always be patient and kind toward my friends. Amen.

In the **Spotlight**

Servant of the Lord: someone who does God's work

What are three things a servant of God must do? You can find the answer in the devotion.

Search **LIGHT**

Bright IDEA

Plan some activities that you and a friend can do together to practice getting along. Work a puzzle, build something, or do a craft. Remember to be kind and patient with one another.

Shine your LIGHT

You and your friends can be bright, shining servants who reflect God's love. Promise each other that you will always do your best to get along. Then help others to get along too by reminding them that a servant of the Lord should be patient and kind.

Hi, Neighbor!

Someone asked Jesus, "What is the greatest commandment of all?" Jesus answered, "Love God with all your heart—and love your neighbors."

When Jesus said, "Love your neighbors," He wasn't talking just about the people who live next door or across the street. Jesus meant that the whole world is your neighborhood, and everyone in it is your neighbor. One of the best ways to shine your love for God is to be a good neighbor to everyone. When you put on your thinking cap, you will find all sorts of ways to help your neighbors near and far.

Look around you. Are there people on your street who are sick or old? Ask your mom and dad what you can do to help them. Watch for activities your community offers to help others. You and your family can join in. You can donate clothing and food to people in need. Maybe your church knows of ways to help needy people around the world. Your youth pastor or Bible class teacher might have ideas about how you can help.

When you behave like a good neighbor to everyone, you make others feel good, and you feel good too!

In the **Spotlight**

Commandment: a very important rule

Sparkling **SCRIPTURE**

"Jesus answered, 'Love the Lord your God with all your heart, soul and mind.' This is the first and most important command. And the second command is like the first: 'Love your neighbor as you love yourself.'"

MATTHEW 22:37–39

Shine your LIGHT

Adopt a neighbor! With your family, choose one neighbor, near or far, whom your family will help this month. Talk about how you will help the person. Cut out a heart from construction paper, and write the person's name on it. Display it on the fridge or bulletin board so you won't forget.

You Go First!

When Emily came home from school, she saw that the family dog, Max, had made a big mess. He got into the garbage and dumped everything out on the kitchen floor. Banana peels, dirty paper towels, chicken bones, and parts of last night's supper were everywhere. *Oh well,* Emily thought. *Mom hasn't seen it yet. I'll leave it for her to clean up.*

Selfishness is when you leave the hard or messy work to others. It's when you push your way to the front and say, "Me first." Selfish people care only about their own feelings, not about the feelings of others.

Jesus was never selfish. Every day He worked hard for everyone. Even when He felt tired and wanted to rest, He put doing for others before doing for Himself. That's the way He wants us to live—always sharing and caring.

When Emily saw the mess that Max made, she could have cleaned it up for her mom. Instead, she put herself first and did what *she* wanted to do.

If you were Emily, what would you have done?

Act out these scenes with a friend to show what you would do to be sharing and caring.

Bright IDEA

* *Your mom made some healthy and yummy granola bars. There is one left, and you and your sister both want it.*

* *You and your friend are at the zoo. You both want to go on the camel ride, but only one kid can ride the camel at a time.*

* *Your older brother isn't feeling well. It's his day to take out the garbage, and the trash can is full.*

Shine your LIGHT

Give up one evening this week to make cards or draw pictures for people who live in a nursing home. Ask a grown-up to call the nursing home to see when you can bring the cards. When you are at the nursing home, ask about other ways that you can help brighten the lives of those who live there.

I Love You More

Brothers and sisters fight sometimes. After all, you're together every single day, and sometimes you are going to lose your cool. But that doesn't mean you shouldn't love one another. God put brothers and sisters together in families for a reason. Jesus said that no one could hate their brothers and sisters and love God too. God put brothers and sisters together so they can practice loving. They are like a sports team practicing to play a game really well. When players mess up in practice, they try again and learn to do better. When you learn to get along, share, and talk nicely to your brothers and sisters, then you take what you learn into the world and act loving toward everyone you meet. And God likes that, because love spreads His light around.

God also likes it when you share lots of love with your brothers and sisters. Say, "I love you," once in a while. And if your brother and sister tell you they love you, answer back, "I love you more!"

You may not always get along, but your brothers and sisters will always be your family. As you get older, it's likely that you will become even closer and be best friends forever.

Bright **IDEA**

Set aside a special time each week to do a fun activity with just your brothers and sisters. You could play a game, read books to each other, do an art project, or have a picnic. What other fun things can you think of to do?

Dear *God*

Thank You for my brothers and sisters. Forgive me for the times I don't get along with them, and help me to try harder. Amen.

Shine your LIGHT

Do secret, loving things this week for your brothers and sisters. Try not to get caught. You could make their beds, pick up their rooms, and leave little treats for them. When they figure out that it's you, smile and say, "I did it because I love you!"

Thank You, God, for My Parents

Mom: Callie, it's time to set the dinner table.

Callie: I'm busy. You do it.

Can you imagine talking back to your mom that way? Parents are God's gift to children, and He wants children to respect their parents. God put parents in families to love, protect, comfort, and teach their children. He gave parents wisdom to help their kids grow into good Christian adults someday. To answer your mother the way Callie did would make God very unhappy.

Jesus shows us how to treat our parents. He never, ever disobeyed His Father. He listened to God, trusted Him, and didn't talk back. Jesus always spoke with and about His Father with respect.

There will be times when you won't feel like respecting your parents or following their rules. When that happens, ask God to help you, and He will help change your attitude. Maybe you don't live with your mom or dad all the time. God wants you to honor and respect the other grown-ups who help parent you too. When you obey God by honoring your parents, your life will be happier—and so will theirs.

In the **Spotlight**

Honor: to be respectful of someone

Sparkling **SCRIPTURE**

"Children, obey your parents the way the Lord wants. This is the right thing to do."

EPHESIANS 6:1

Bright IDEA

Someday you might be a parent. How would you want your children to honor and respect you? Play this game with your parents: switch places for one hour. You pretend to be the parent, and they pretend to be your kids . . . just don't ask to drive the car! Afterward, talk about it. Is it easy being a parent? Is it easy being a kid?

Shine your LIGHT

One way to honor your parents is to volunteer to help around the house. Volunteering means doing without being asked. Find two ways to help your parents today.

Come on Over!

You and your best friend are playing in your front yard. A big moving van pulls up a few houses away. Men unload furniture and boxes, and you see a girl about your age standing nearby, watching them. You haven't seen her before, and she looks lonely. She's the new kid! You and your best friend could invite her over to play. Then you could help her meet your other friends, and you could all have fun playing together.

Sometimes it's hard for new kids to make friends. That's why you should be on the lookout for new kids or lonely kids and make them feel welcome. Wherever Jesus went, many people welcomed Him, and that's how you should welcome others.

Everyone wants to fit in, and

everyone needs friends. Do you know a kid in your neighborhood or school who is new or doesn't have many friends? Be kind, welcoming, and caring. You never know—a new friend might become a best friend. You don't need just one friend, or two friends, or three. The more friends you have, the better!

Bright IDEA

A tea party is a wonderful way to welcome new friends. You can make pretty invitations and decorations for the table. Little sandwiches and cookies are perfect to serve with tea. And if the weather is good, you can have your party outside.

Shine your LIGHT

Try to make one new friend this week. Smile and say something nice to a kid in school or in Bible class whom you don't know very well—someone whom you think might be a friend. You could say something kind about what she is wearing—"Those are really cool socks!"—or about something she does well—"You're a very good dancer!" As you get to know one another better, maybe you can have a playdate together.

I Forgive You

One of Jesus' helpers came to Him and asked, "If someone does wrong things to me, how many times do I have to forgive him? Is seven times enough?" Jesus answered, "Not seven times, but seventy times seven."

Seventy times seven is 490, and that's a whole lot of forgiving! Jesus wants us to keep forgiving over and over, just like He does.

When someone does wrong to you, you might spend a lot of time thinking about it and feeling hurt and angry. We all feel bad when someone hurts us. But, often, the people who hurt us feel bad too.

The good news is that God allows "do-overs." A do-over is when you decide to forgive someone and start fresh. When you forgive, then you are acting just like Jesus, and that's what God wants.

Of course, if someone keeps being mean to you and isn't sorry, you shouldn't just stand there and take it. Hurting people is never okay! Walk away and tell a grown-up. The important thing to remember is when people keep doing wrong to you, you should forgive them in your heart. Forgiveness makes your heart feel better.

In the **Spotlight**

Forgive: to let go of your bad feelings toward others

When someone isn't sorry for hurting you, you should still forgive him in your heart. Draw a picture of what happened and how it made you feel. The Bible tells us not to keep track of the wrong things people do to us, so tear up your paper into little pieces. Pretend that you are tearing up all those hurt feelings. Forgiveness is God's gift to us to help us live in a world that is not fair.

Shine your LIGHT

Has someone hurt your feelings? Ask God to help you forgive that person. Ask Him to take away the hurt and fill up your heart with His love.

Sometimes I Don't Like You, but I Do Love You

By the time she got home from school, Sophia was crying.

"What's the matter?" her mom asked.

"Taylor is mean to me, and she says mean things about me to other people. I hate her!"

"Do you *really* hate Taylor?" her mom asked. "Would Jesus hate her?"

When Sophia thought about it, she knew that Jesus wouldn't hate Taylor. He would love her even if she was mean. Jesus said we should love our enemies.

"But it's hard sometimes!" Sophia said.

God knows it's hard. He understands that Taylor had a bad attitude, and it wasn't Sophia's fault. Still, God doesn't want

Sophia to be mean and fight back. He wants her to treat Taylor with kindness. Jesus says that we are to love our enemies and pray for them. When we treat difficult people with kindness, it's like shining God's light on them. We show them how much God loves them by loving them ourselves.

When you are kind and pray for your enemies, you have faith that God will change their hearts someday. Who knows? Maybe your prayers and kindness will lead them to Jesus. Wouldn't that be wonderful?

Sparkling **SCRIPTURE**

"Love your enemies. Pray for those who hurt you."

Matthew 5:44

Sophia found it hard to like Taylor, but she knew that Jesus said, "Love your enemies." How can Sophia show God's love to Taylor the next time she sees her?

Search LIGHT

Bright IDEA

You will need some bubble liquid and a bubble wand. Blow some bubbles into the air. Pretend they are your enemies and you are sending them to God for help. Say a prayer for your enemies, and ask God to bless them.

Shine your LIGHT

Sit down with your family and choose one difficult person you all know. Pray for the person, and then work together to make a special treat (maybe some cookies) to give to him or her. Include a kind note. Sharing a treat may not change the person, but your kindness will please God.

Helping Friends
Near and Far

*E*arthquakes and storms happen all around the world, and sometimes they leave people without a home and needing help. That's when God sends in His army. Christians are like a big army for God. When they see that people have lost their houses and everything they own, they step right up and help.

When something happens on the other side of the country, or even the other side of the world, you don't have to go there to help. There are things you can do from home. Kids can help by earning money and giving it to their church or to service groups. Some donate their allowances or what they collect from lemonade stands or bake sales. Others donate money they get from collecting cans and taking them to recycling centers.

Helpers ask for money so they can provide food, water, and clothing for people. Money is used to help people in hospitals, to rebuild homes and schools, and even to buy books and Bibles. You don't have to give a lot to make a difference— even a little bit helps. Your pennies, nickels, dimes, and quarters will be added to those from other kids to make lots of dollars to help those in need.

Sparkling **SCRIPTURE**

"Being kind to the poor is like lending to the Lord. The Lord will reward you for what you have done."

Proverbs 19:17

In the **Spotlight**

Donate: to give something to others

When an earthquake happened on the other side of the world, some kids made posters to put up at church, school, and other places. Their posters reminded people to help out. You can do the same! The next time you hear about a storm or earthquake that leaves people needing help, make some posters. It's a great way to spread the word and get many people to help.

Shine your LIGHT

Set up a family piggy bank to help people in need.
Whenever you have a few extra pennies, nickels,
or dimes, put them in the bank. You
will be surprised by how fast the
coins add up. Then the next time
an earthquake or storm happens,
your family will be ready to
help out.

Just the Way You Are

Can you imagine a world where everybody looks exactly alike? What a crazy, mixed-up world that would be! You wouldn't know which friend you were playing with or which mom was yours. Teachers, doctors, bus drivers—everyone would be the same.

God didn't make His world that way. He made each person different. Some have black hair and brown eyes; others have brown hair and blue eyes. Skin comes in all shades from light tan to dark brown. Some people wear glasses, and others don't. Some walk, and others use wheelchairs. Everybody is different in one way or another, and you are too.

Jesus loves everyone, no matter how they look, walk, or talk. He wants you to love them too. Just because someone is different from you doesn't mean you should make fun of him or her or think that you are better. Instead, remember

Jesus' Golden Rule: "Act toward others exactly the way that you want them to act toward you." The Bible tells us that loving each other brings glory to God. It makes His light shine bright and strong. So, celebrate being different. It's what makes each person God's special, one-of-a-kind creation.

You will need:

* *Two big pieces of white butcher paper*
* *Crayons*

Do this with a friend. Have your friend lie on her back on the butcher paper while you trace around her. Then have her trace around you. Now trade papers and finish the pictures of each other. As you draw and color, notice the ways that God made you and your friend different. If you want to, write on your picture *I Like You Just the Way You Are.*

Search LIGHT

People know you by your name. It's one thing that is special about you. You will have it for the rest of your life. Ask your mom or dad how they chose your name and what makes it special.

Shine your LIGHT

Do you know someone who is teased because he or she is different? Reach out to that person, and be kind. Along with showing him or her how God loves us all, you might get a brand-new friend!

Always and Forever

*H*ere is a little riddle for you. What comes from Jesus, you keep it in your heart, and it never stops working? The answer is *love*! Jesus' love is in your heart forever. It always works to make you a better person and the world a better place.

Think of the person you love the most and how very much you love him or her. Jesus loves you more. Stretch out your arms and say, "I love you this big!" Jesus loves you a gazillion times more than that. His love for you is so big that you could never measure it no matter how hard you tried. The best part is that His love never ends. It lasts forever. Jesus loved you before you were born, He

has loved you every day since, and He loves you now. He will love you every day of your life, and after that forever. Jesus' love will never let you down. His love is like one big circle that just keeps going 'round and 'round and 'round.

Bright IDEA

Help spread Jesus' forever love by sharing it. Draw a picture or write a poem for someone you love.

Dear *Jesus*

Thank You that no matter what I do, where I go, or how old I am, Your love for me will last forever. Amen.

Find and read 1 John 3:1 in your Bible. Then see if you can finish this sentence. God loves us so much that He calls us His

Search **LIGHT**

_____.

Shine your LIGHT

Have fun with your family making a "Jesus Loves You" time capsule. Use a large plastic box with a tight lid. Each family member should put something into the box that stands for Jesus' forever love (Bible verses, pictures, poems, a

cross—whatever you can think of). Add a letter telling about the time capsule and Jesus' forever love. Don't forget to include the date. Now put your time capsule in a plastic bag to protect it even more, and ask your parents to help you bury it somewhere in your yard. Say a prayer that someday someone will dig it up and learn about Jesus' never-ending love from it.

Something That Can't Be Taken Away

*T*rue or false? When you misbehave, God doesn't love you anymore. Did you say, "False"? Good for you! God *always* loves you, no matter what. His love for you can never be taken away.

Sin is in our world, and where there is sin, people are sometimes pulled toward it. There are times when everyone misbehaves. That's because nobody is perfect. The only perfect One is God. He understands that you will mess up sometimes. When you do, He forgives you. His love for you is perfect, and it will never change.

God's love is everywhere. Nothing can stop it. Love is the most super of all God's superpowers. The Bible says, "Nothing above us, nothing below us, or anything else in the whole world will ever be able to separate us from the love of God" (Romans 8:39). God's love is everyday, all day, forever love. He sees when you misbehave, He knows your secrets, and He loves you anyway.

God doesn't want you to misbehave, but when you do, ask Him to forgive you. He will. Then tell Him that you love Him, because He loves you—always!

Sparkling SCRIPTURE

"Nothing above us, nothing below us, or anything else in the whole world will ever be able to separate us from the love of God."

Romans 8:39

Bright
IDEA

Circles are everywhere. A happy face, pizza, DVD, and basketball hoop are all circles. Look around you for other circles. Count how many you find. Did you notice that circles have no beginning or end? That's how it is with God's love. It goes on forever.

Shine your LIGHT

On a piece of heavy paper, trace a circle using a clean metal or plastic jar lid about 2 inches wide. Write *God always loves you!* on the circle, cut it out, and glue it inside the lid. Give your jar-lid message to a friend. Tell her to keep it going by passing it on to another person and telling that person to pass it on again. Who knows where God's love message will go? Maybe all the way around the world!

Joy! Joy! Joy!

*J*oy! Whoo-hoo! It makes you want to sing and dance. Joy is a wonderful gift from God. It is happiness that comes from deep in your heart and shines outward to everyone you meet.

God fills up your heart with joy so you can praise Him. In Bible times, people praised God by singing, dancing, and playing musical instruments. They sounded their trumpets, flutes, and harps and clashed their cymbals, all making joyful, happy music to the Lord. We do the same thing today when we sing to God and play songs for Him in church.

Praise is a special way of celebrating God's love and thanking Him for His goodness and greatness. It isn't just about singing, dancing, and making music. Praise is also telling God in your prayers that He is wonderful. When you see something amazing that He made, you can say, "Wow, God, You are so great!" When He helps you solve a problem, you can say, "God, You are awesome!" Get in the habit of telling God, over and over, just how much You love Him. Praise Him, and feel your heart fill up with joy.

In the Spotlight

Praise: joyfully thanking God for His greatness

In Bible times, horns were used to praise the Lord. Here's how to make a praise horn.

You will need:

* A cardboard paper towel roll

* A piece of waxed paper big enough to cover one end of the roll

* A rubber band

* A pen

Close up one end of the paper towel roll by placing the waxed paper over it. Use the rubber band to hold it in place. Use the pen to punch 3 to 5 holes in a straight line along the side of the tube. Now hum into the open side of the tube to make music. You can change how it sounds by covering some of the holes with your fingers. Praise God with your music even if your dog covers his ears!

Bright IDEA

Dear God

You are an
amazing,
wonderful, and
loving God.
Thank You for
Your greatness
and blessings.
I love You,
God. Amen.

Shine your LIGHT

Get together with your friends and make up a joyful song or a dance to praise God. Spread the joy around by performing it for others. Ask your audience to join with you in praising the Lord. Can you think of other ways to praise God?

Peace in My Heart

Do you sometimes feel worried and stressed-out? Many kids do. You might be worried about something at school or at home. Whatever it is, Jesus has an answer for it. He said, "Don't worry. Look at the birds. God knows everything they do, and He cares for them. If God takes care of birds, then He definitely takes care of you." Jesus always knew the right things to say. Everything He said was true and trustworthy.

Another name for Jesus is "Prince of Peace." Before Jesus went back up to heaven to be with God, He said, "Peace I leave with you." Jesus' peace can be with you in your heart always, even on days when you are worried or upset. Like God, Jesus is always there loving you and wanting to help you.

Whenever you feel troubled, you can always ask Jesus to bring you some peace. He cares about kids and their problems. When you believe in Jesus and remember His peace in your heart, then you will begin to feel less worried and afraid.

In the **Spotlight**

Peace: feeling quiet inside, without upsetting thoughts and feelings

Dear Jesus

Sometimes I feel worried and afraid. When I feel that way, please help me remember that You love me and that You will take care of me. Amen.

Bright IDEA

Get a small box and decorate it with things that remind you of Jesus. Whenever you have a problem, write it on a piece of paper and put it into the box. Imagine that you are giving the problem to Jesus so you won't need to worry about it anymore. Invite your family to put their problems into the box too.

Shine your LIGHT

You share Christ's peace when you act in ways that are gentle, kind, and caring. Maybe you know someone who is afraid of trying something new. If you know that someone is afraid, you can encourage her not to worry and remind her that Jesus will take care of her.

Practicing Patience

GENESIS 17:15–19; 21:1–7

One day God told Abram to pack all his things and go with his wife, Sarai, to a new, faraway place. Abram always obeyed God, so he and his family packed up and went. God told Abram that someday, after they got to their new home, He would bless them with children and Abram's family would grow and grow.

Years passed. Abram and Sarai grew old, and they still didn't have any children! You can imagine that Abram was getting impatient. Then one night God told him, "Go outside and try to count all the stars. That is how many children, grandchildren, and great-great-grandchildren you will have someday." Of course there were too many stars for Abram to count.

Abram trusted God. He went on trying to be patient, but he wondered how two old people, like himself and Sarai, could have children.

After all, babies are usually born to much younger couples.

Then one day, when Abram was almost a hundred years old, God was ready. He gave Abram and Sarai new names—Abraham and Sarah. God told Abraham that soon Sarah would have a baby boy, and they should name him Isaac. Abraham laughed and said to himself, "Sarah is ninety years old! That's too old to have a baby." And when Sarah heard about it, she laughed too.

But God always keeps His promises. After about a year, Abraham and Sarah did have a baby boy. They named him Isaac, which means "he laughs." They had waited many years for their child. They had even laughed, thinking that they couldn't have kids in their old age. But God rewarded their patience and gave them a baby. Sarah said, "God has brought me laughter, and everyone who hears this story will laugh with joy! Who would have thought that I would have a baby at this old age?"

When Isaac grew up, he had kids, and they had kids, and Abraham's family grew and grew.

When you have trouble being patient, you can remember the story of Abraham and Sarah. Abraham trusted God. By trusting God, we learn patience. Sometimes God asks us to be patient for a long time. We shouldn't complain because He is always very patient with us. Think about the times you misbehaved and God waited patiently for you to do better. He wants you to be just as patient with Him as He is with you.

In the Spotlight

Patience: waiting peacefully without complaining

If you were there...

If God promised you something but it would take years for you to get it, would you be patient like Abram? Why or why not?

Shine your LIGHT

Being patient with others is another way to shine your light. If your parents ask you to wait, be patient. If your brothers and sisters get on your nerves, be patient. As you practice, your patience will grow and grow—just like Abraham's family!

Little Sparks of Kindness

*Y*our mom is having a busy day. Dishes are piled in the sink, and loads of dirty clothes need to be washed. There's cleaning to do and dinner to be made. Your mom didn't get to any of it because she took you shopping and then to your dance lesson, and after that she treated you to ice cream. What can you do to show her some kindness?

Kindness doesn't have to be a big deal. You can shine your light with little sparks of kindness. Your mom would love it if you helped her by picking up your things without being asked. You could also play nicely with your little brother or sister while Mom does her work. If you think really hard, you can come up with loads of little ways to be kind.

The Bible says that kindness is one way to show God's love. Jesus showed great kindness to people wherever He went. He was kind to people who didn't like Him and even to those who didn't thank Him for His kindness. And that's how you should be. Do kind little things for people straight from your heart—it makes God happy!

 Please open my eyes to see the little sparks of kindness all around me. Then show me how to be kind to others. Amen.

Sparkling **SCRIPTURE**

"Be kind and loving to each other."

Ephesians 4:32

Be on the lookout today for little sparks of kindness. When you see someone being kind, write it down. At the end of the day, count up all those little acts of kindness.

Shine your LIGHT

Little sparks of kindness are just that—little! Thinking of and praying for someone is kindness. So is saying thank you to someone who usually doesn't get thanked, like a police officer, mail carrier, crossing guard, or teacher. Helping someone in any little way is kindness. So be kind. Let those little sparks shine.

Glowing Goodness

*H*ave you heard someone say, "God is always good"? Just like His love for you, God's goodness is everywhere. Think of filling a glass with water and letting the faucet run forever so the cup keeps overflowing. That's what God's goodness is like. He keeps filling up your heart with a goodness that never ends.

True goodness is doing what God wants you to do. God gave very special rules to His people, and you can use them as a guide for being good. They are called *The Ten Commandments.*

* Put God first.
* Worship only God.
* Only say God's name with respect.
* Remember that Sunday is God's special day.
* Honor your father and mother.
* Do not kill.

- When you get married, keep your marriage promises.
- Do not steal.
- Do not lie.
- Do not be jealous of what others have.

The neat thing about God's goodness is that it spills out of us to other people. When you behave in ways that are pleasing to God, other people see, and they might follow your good example. That's how you spread God's goodness to everyone you meet!

Search LIGHT

Which is commandment number 4?
What do you think it means?

Shine your LIGHT

Practice this little saying: "God is always good. Always God is good." Then do your best to always be good for God. Whenever you obey God's rules, you shine your light for Him.

Fiery Faith

DANIEL 3

King Nebuchadnezzar didn't worship the one true God. Instead, he had his men make a big golden statue. The king had a rule that whenever his subjects heard music play, they had to bow down and worship the statue. If they didn't, they would be thrown into a fiery furnace. Most people obeyed the king because they were afraid. No one wanted to be tossed into a fire!

There were three men, Shadrach, Meshach, and Abednego, who loved God. No way would they bow down to that statue! The king warned them and gave them another chance. But they said, "No, our God is able to save us from the fiery furnace. If He decides not to save us, we still worship the one true God." That made the king really mad. He ordered the fire to be made seven times hotter, and then his men threw Shadrach, Meshach, and Abednego into the furnace!

When King Nebuchadnezzar saw what happened next, he couldn't believe his eyes. "Didn't you throw just three men into the furnace?" he asked. "I see four men in the fire walking around, and they all seem fine!"

Then the king called Shadrach, Meshach, and Abednego to come out. When he saw that not even one hair on their heads had been burned, the king knew that their faith had saved them. God was the fourth man in the fire, and He had protected Shadrach, Meshach, and Abednego from the flames. Now the king understood how powerful it is to have faith, and he made a new rule that no one should ever say anything bad about the one true God.

The story of Shadrach, Meshach, and Abednego shows that faith is stronger than fear. When you believe with all your heart that God is with you, He helps make you strong. Jesus had faith to go where people hated Him and do God's work. Faith made Jesus strong when He died on the cross for our sins. Whenever He faced something bad, Jesus didn't give up. He had faith that God was with Him.

Do you have faith that God is always with you? He is! God is everywhere, just like the air you breathe.

If *you* were there...

Would you have worshipped the king's golden statue, or would you have said no like Shadrach, Meshach, and Abednego did?

Sparkling SCRIPTURE

"Faith means being sure of the things we hope for. And faith means knowing that something is real even if we do not see it."

HEBREWS 11:1

Shine your LIGHT

Make a faith patch to wear on your clothes.

You'll need:

- A piece of heavy white paper, or cardboard at least 6 inches square
- Crayons
- A small piece of double-sided tape

Cut a circle from the paper or cardboard about 4 inches across. (You could trace around a glass or other round object to make the circle.)

Write the word FAITH on your patch. Then decorate it any way you want.

Put the piece of tape on the back. Now you can stick it on your shirt! When your friends ask about your patch, you can tell them all about having faith in the one true God.

Loving God's Creatures

*I*n the beginning, God made all the creatures that live on earth and in the water: bugs, dogs, fish, cats, hamsters, birds— every kind of animal that you can imagine. All of them belonged to God. He put the first humans, Adam and Eve, in charge as His special animal helpers. It was their job to care for the animals.

God wants you to be His animal helper too. You can shine God's light on animals all around you by taking good care of them.

At home, you can make sure your pets have food and water and that their places are clean. Just like kids, pets don't like to be yelled at or told to go away. Your job is to remember that and be kind to them all the time.

Wild animals in your neighborhood need help too. Wild birds like fresh water and birdseed. Butterflies like being looked at but not touched or put in jars. It is important to remember that you should never touch a wild animal. If you see an animal in trouble, you can help by calling an adult.

The most important part of being God's animal helper is to be gentle like Jesus was. The Bible compares Jesus to a gentle shepherd. Jesus took care of people the same way a kind shepherd cares for his sheep. Jesus always acted in ways that were calm, wise, and loving. When you are gentle with animals, like Jesus was with people, you shine God's light on them and make the world a better place for them to live in.

The Bible says that a good person takes care of her animals (Proverbs 12:10). That good person is you! Can you think of some other ways to be kind to animals?

Search LIGHT

Spend some time sitting quietly in your yard or a park. How many different birds do you see? Now walk around and look for bugs. Did you find some different ones? Are there wild animals around, like squirrels or bunnies?

Dear Jesus

Help me to be gentle like You are and to be a good helper to God's animals. Amen.

Bright IDEA

Which is your favorite wild animal? Draw a picture of it. Try to find out more about it. Where does it live? What does it eat? What would be a good name for it? If God put you in charge of it, what would you do to help it survive?

Shine your LIGHT

Ask your parents to call your local animal shelter and find out ways you can help. Maybe you can collect pet food or old towels to give to the shelter. Or you might be able to help walk dogs and care for the animals while they wait for new homes.

Jesus Takes Care of Us

JOHN 6:1–13

*J*esus loved people, and He loved helping them. Sometimes Jesus did miracles— amazing things that no one else could do. He healed the sick and calmed a stormy sea. He even walked on water! Large crowds followed Him wherever He went. People wanted to hear what He said, and they wanted to see what He would do.

One day five thousand people followed Jesus and His disciples up on a mountainside. Jesus knew that they had walked a very long way to see Him and that they were very, very hungry. "Where can we buy enough bread for them to eat?" Jesus asked His disciples.

"It would cost much more money than we have," they answered.

Then one disciple, Andrew, said, "I see a boy over there with five small loaves of bread and two small fish. But how far will that go among all these people?"

Jesus already knew how far it would go. He had everyone sit down on the grass. Then He asked the boy to share his bread and fish. Jesus said a prayer to thank God for the bread. He passed the bread out to all the people, and He did the same with the boy's two small fish. There was enough food for everyone! Jesus made a miracle—five loaves and two fish fed five thousand people! When the people had eaten and were full, Jesus told His disciples to gather up all the leftovers, and they filled up twelve more baskets.

What a miracle! Jesus knew what the people needed, and He used His amazing power to take care of those He loved. Jesus makes sure you have everything you need too. Taking care of us is just one of the ways He shows how much He loves you.

Sparkling SCRIPTURE

"Don't worry and say, 'What will we eat?' or 'What will we drink?' or 'What will we wear?' All the people who don't know God keep trying to get these things. And your Father in heaven knows that you need them."

MATTHEW 6:31–32

Dear Jesus

I think it is amazing that You always know what I need and take care of me. Please show me how I can help others too. Amen.

Shine your LIGHT

Jesus fed five thousand hungry people. You can shine your light by helping the hungry too! You can

* donate food to a food pantry,
* help with a food drive, or
* check with a homeless shelter to find out if you can bake something or make soup or sandwiches for the people they help.

What other ways can you think of to help?

God Helps When I Am Afraid

There was a time, long ago, when God's people were afraid of a giant. His name was Goliath, and he was nine feet tall. Goliath was mean too. "Come on and fight with me!" he roared. Goliath looked so scary dressed in his armor that no one wanted to fight him.

A boy named David came along and saw Goliath shouting and acting crazy. God's people were so afraid that they wanted to run away, but David stayed right there. "Don't let that big bully scare you," David told them. "He's nothing to be afraid of." Then David did something dangerous but brave. He got out his slingshot and picked up some stones. He marched right up to Goliath, who was growling and yelling and swinging a sword.

"You come at me with a sword, but I come at you in the name of the Lord!" David shouted. "God will help me defeat you!" David trusted God. He put a stone in his slingshot, aimed it at the giant, and let go. The stone hit Goliath smack in the forehead, and he fell facedown on the ground.

David wasn't afraid of Goliath because he knew that God would help him. You might have a problem that seems big and scary, like a giant, but no problem is too big for God. He is always on your side and ready to help.

If *you* were there...

If you were David, what would you say to that mean bully Goliath? What would you do to help you feel brave? God says in His Word, "Don't be afraid. I am with you" (Isaiah 43:5). Remember, God is bigger and stronger than anything that can scare you.

Sparkling SCRIPTURE

"I am the Lord your God. I am holding your right hand. And I tell you, 'Don't be afraid. I will help you.'"

Isaiah 41:13

Bright IDEA

Moms, dads, grandparents, kids—everyone is afraid sometimes. What are you afraid of? Draw a picture of it. Then, on a separate piece of paper, write "GOD" in large letters and glue or tape the piece of paper over the scary picture to remind you that God is greater than anything that makes you feel afraid.

Dear Jesus

Whenever I feel afraid, help me to trust You. I believe that You love me so much and that You will always come to help me. Amen.

Shine your LIGHT

Make a list of ways you can help a friend or a younger brother or sister who feels afraid. You can act silly and make him laugh. You can tell her the story of David and Goliath and remind her that God can make her brave. And you can say a prayer with him. Let your light shine by bringing a smile to the faces of people you love.

Best Friends in Good Times and Bad Times

*J*esus is perfect in every way. When He lived on earth, He never sinned, and He was a best friend to everyone who believed in Him. He was a friend to them in good times and bad.

Jesus is your best friend too. If you try to act like He did, you will become more and more like Him. You can't be perfect like Jesus is, but you can try your very best to behave like Him and be a good role model for others.

Asking Jesus into your heart as your very best friend is a wise choice. He is a friend who truly loves you and will never let you down. You should make the same wise choices about all your friends. There is a verse in the Bible that says, "A friend loves you all the time" (Proverbs 17:17). That is the kind of friend that Jesus wants you to be. He wants you to love your friends through good times and bad, just like He does, and He wants you to choose friends who will do the same for you. You should always be a good role model for your friends by behaving in ways that would please Jesus.

Choose friends who love Jesus the same way you do. Then you can have fun sharing Jesus with each other, and together you can tell other kids all about Him.

Sparkling **SCRIPTURE**

"You are my friends if you do what I command you."

John 15:14

Make a Jesus friendship bracelet!
You will need:

- ❋ *A white cardboard strip 2 inches wide and long enough to wrap around your wrist*
- ❋ *Crayons or markers and stickers or other decorations*
- ❋ *Tape*

Write *Jesus Is My Friend* on the cardboard. Then decorate the cardboard any way you want. When you are finished, have someone wrap it around your wrist and tape it. Wear your bracelet to remind you that Jesus is your very best friend.

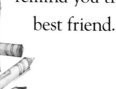

Shine your LIGHT

Do you know that you are a role model? You are! Other kids see how you behave. You can be a good role model or a bad one. A bad role model doesn't care how she behaves, but a good role model tries to behave like Jesus. You can shine your light everywhere you go by being a good role model for Him.

Anyone Can Change

ACTS 9:1–30

*A*fter Jesus died, rose from the dead, and went back up into heaven, a man named Saul fought hard against Jesus' friends. He killed some of them! That's how much Saul hated Jesus. One day Saul was walking along a road, thinking of more ways to bully Christians. Then suddenly a very bright light came down from heaven. It made Saul blind, and he fell to the ground. Jesus' voice came from inside the light. "Saul, Saul, why are you hurting those who love Me?"

Saul was so afraid. "Jesus," he said, "what do You want from me?"

"Go into the city and wait," Jesus said.

So Saul's friends helped him to the city. He waited there for three days and prayed that he would be able to see again.

Then Jesus told His friend Ananias to go to Saul. Jesus gave Ananias some of His very

special power to fix Saul's eyes.
Ananias put his hands on
Saul, and an amazing thing
happened. Stuff that looked like
fish scales fell off Saul's eyes. He
could see again!

Saul felt so thankful and full of God's
light that he gave up bullying Christians. God changed his
name to Paul, and he spent the rest of his life telling the
world all about God. Saul's story shows that anyone can
change. Jesus didn't give up on Saul when he behaved in
such a mean way. Jesus loved him and wanted him to be a
better person. You shouldn't give up on friends who don't
believe in Jesus either. Keep on praying that someday Jesus
will turn their lives around, just like He did for Saul.

In the **Spotlight**

Christian: a person who believes in Jesus and the things He says and does

Search **LIGHT**

After Saul became one of Jesus' followers, he changed his name. What was Saul's new name? You will find the answer in the devotion.

Shine your LIGHT

You can shine Jesus' light on friends who don't believe. Pray for them, and tell them about Jesus. Invite them to go to church with you so they can learn more about Jesus and the Bible.

God's Perfect Gifts

*E*veryone loves getting gifts. Some are small and some are big. Some last a little while and others last a long time. Some gifts are extra special, come from above, and last forever—they are God's blessings.

You can't see God's blessings coming down from heaven, but they are there, just like God is. His blessings shower down on you every day. There are so many blessings that you can't count them all.

God's blessings are things you might not think of, and each one is a perfect gift. God blesses you with family and friends to love you and a body that lets you work and play. He gives you food to eat, a home to live in, and clothes to keep your body protected and warm. He makes wonderful places for you to visit and amazing things for you to see. Anything good that you can think of is a blessing, a perfect gift from God to you.

God never stops giving gifts to His children. He loves giving you everything you need with a lot of happiness and joy mixed in. Can you think of times when God has given you something? When you say your prayers tonight, remember to thank Him for all of His wonderful blessings.

Sparkling **SCRIPTURE**

"Every good action and every perfect gift is from God."

James 1:17

Bright IDEA

Share this game with your family or friends. Sit in a circle and take turns rolling or tossing a ball to each other. When you get the ball, you have ten seconds to name one of God's blessings. You must name a blessing that another player has not named. When players can't think of a blessing in ten seconds or less, they're out. Who is the best at remembering all God's blessings?

Dear God

Thank You for Your gifts and especially for giving me people who love me. As I fall asleep tonight, remind me of all my blessings. Amen.

Shine your LIGHT

Every time you show kindness to others, even in a small way, God blesses them through your actions. So be a helper, be a good sport, and be a good friend—be a blessing to everyone you meet.

Quiet Time with the Lord

*K*aylee was so excited when she got home from her friend Riley's sleepover. "Mom," Kaylee said. "Riley's family has quiet time with the Lord!"

Riley's family gets together every night before bedtime to read from the Bible and talk about Jesus. At the sleepover, Riley's dad told stories from the Bible, and he explained to the girls why their family loves Jesus. Then they sang worship songs and said a prayer together before everyone went to sleep.

"Can we do that too, Mom?" Kaylee asked.

Kaylee's mother agreed that quiet time with the Lord was a good idea.

Quiet time with the Lord sometimes includes the whole family, but it can also be time you spend alone with Jesus reading your Bible, praying, or just being still and thinking about

Him. The important thing is to set aside a special time each day to spend with the Lord. Spending quiet time with Him helps you learn more about Him and love Him even more.

Sparkling **SCRIPTURE**

*"Come near to God, and God
will come near to you."*

<small>JAMES 4:8</small>

Help me to sit quietly and spend time with You. Calm down my thoughts and speak to my heart. Amen.

Ask your parents if you can have a journal where you can write or draw your thoughts about Jesus. You can also use your journal to write letters to Jesus and to list the names of people you pray for.

Shine your LIGHT

Be like Kaylee, and suggest that your family spend some quiet time with the Lord. Set aside a special time each day when you can sit together to learn about Jesus and the Bible.

Use Your Gifts to Praise Him

*W*hat are you really good at doing? Maybe you dance or sing or play a sport. You might be good at solving problems, writing stories, or drawing. God gives everyone a talent—something they do very well.

The Bible says that whatever you do, you should work at it with all your heart as if you are doing it for the Lord. Sharing your talent with others is a special way of praising Him. If you play a sport, you can praise God by playing your best for Him and thanking Him whether you win or lose. If you sing or dance you can do it as if performing for the Lord. If you are creative, you can write stories or draw pictures about Jesus and share them with others. If you are good at a subject in school, you can help kids who don't understand the subject as well.

Praising God means giving Him all the credit. Think about your special talents. If someone says to you, "Good job!" you could answer, "God gets the praise." If you win at a game, you could say, "Praise God for helping me!"

What is your special talent? How can you use it to praise the Lord?

Bright
IDEA

You might have to put on your thinking cap to find your special talents. Are you a good reader? Are you a good helper? Do you make amazing peanut butter and jelly sandwiches? Everyone is good at something. Make a list of the things you are good at. Then give the Lord praise, and thank Him for those things.

Shine your LIGHT

Get your friends together and have a talent show to praise Jesus. You could sing, dance, and tell Bible stories to your audience. Remember that whatever you do, you should do it as if Jesus were your guest of honor. It doesn't have to be perfect. Just the idea that you are doing it for Him is enough.

Say What?

Have you heard someone say something bad about someone else? Maybe one of your friends made fun of Caleb's new haircut. Or your neighbor, Nathan, told everyone that Lexie was a liar. Or one of your classmates told a bunch of kids that Mia failed the spelling test.

God doesn't like any unkind talk—lies, name-calling, angry words, or saying things that make fun of people. Part of shining His light on others is speaking kindly to and about them like Jesus did. Imagine how you would feel if you heard someone saying something bad about you.

You should always think before you speak and only say things that would make others feel good. Tell Caleb you like his new haircut . . . unless it looks like a hedgehog—then just tell him you like *him*! Say something nice about Lexie instead. Encourage Mia when she feels bad. That's the kind of talk that makes God happy!

 **If *you* were there...**

If you heard someone making fun of your friend's new glasses, what would you do? Can you think of a nice way to remind someone to only say kind things about others?

Shine your LIGHT

Have you said something unkind to a friend or family member? Make a card for that person to say, "I'm sorry." Then forgive yourself for what you've said, and try harder next time. God is always ready to forgive and give you another chance.

Let's Play

*G*od filled up the world with all sorts of fun things for kids to see and do. There are playdates and sleepovers, visits to the zoo and the beach, riding bikes, playing at the playground, outside games, pretend games, board games, and so much more!

God wants you to laugh and have fun, but whenever you play and whatever you do, it should be in a way that pleases Him. You should play fair and be kind. You should also be wise about which games you play. If you feel in your heart that God wouldn't approve of a game, then don't play it. Getting along with others when you play is important too. It teaches you to work as a team and to be kind no matter if you win or lose. God doesn't want you to get mad and argue with your friends. When you play well together, it is like shining God's light on each other, and God likes that. When other kids see how nicely you play, they can learn to be good playmates too.

Sparkling SCRIPTURE

"God will yet fill your mouth with laughter. And he will fill your lips with shouts of joy."

Job 8:21

Bright IDEA

Get your friends together for a mural-making party. (A mural is just a really big picture!) You'll need a roll of white butcher paper and plenty of crayons and markers. (You might ask each girl to bring her own.) Before starting, agree on a plan for your mural. What will it be about? Which girl will draw which part? Work as a team to make the mural. Be kind and patient, and play in a way that is pleasing to God.

Shine your LIGHT

Younger brothers and sisters might not be good at some of the games you enjoy playing. Your light will shine brightly if you are patient with them and choose games that they can play too.

Plant a Seed

MATTHEW 13:1–23

*J*esus told this story about a farmer:
One day a farmer went to plant seeds in his field. Some seeds fell on the road, and the birds ate them. Others fell on rocky ground where there wasn't much dirt to grow in. The plants came up, but they died in the hot sun because their roots weren't deep. More seeds fell into tall weeds that squished the plants and kept them from growing. But the seeds the farmer planted in good dirt grew and grew, and before long they made a big crop.

Jesus' followers didn't understand the story, so He explained what it meant.

The seeds that fell on the road are like people who hear what God says in the Bible but the devil steals it from their hearts like birds steal seeds. Those people don't understand or believe in Jesus.

The seeds that fell on the rocky ground are like people who don't allow God's Word to sink deep into their hearts. They are like plants without deep roots. They listen to what God says and then forget about it.

People who think other things are more important than God are like plants that get squished by the weeds. All those other things cover up God's Word and make it seem unimportant.

The people who really listen to and obey God's Word are like plants that grow in good dirt. Their faith grows stronger and stronger, and they serve God by sharing His Word with others.

You can be like the farmer in the story and plant seeds for Jesus. Whenever you share a Bible verse or tell someone about Him, it is like planting a seed in that person's heart. Then you can pray and ask God to make that seed grow big and strong.

In the **Spotlight**

God's Word: everything that is in the Bible

Ask your parents to help you plant a vegetable garden, and give what you grow to a local food pantry. When you plant your seeds, follow the directions on the seed packets. Remember to plant them in a sunny place with good soil. Take care of your garden by pulling out the weeds and giving the plants plenty of water.

Shine your LIGHT

Share your favorite Bible verse with one person today. Tell him or her to share it with one other person and to ask that person to pass it on. Pray that the verse you shared will keep going and growing in people's hearts.

Yes, You Can!

Sydney went to a party at a roller-skating rink. She and most of her friends were having fun skating when she saw Kara sitting on a chair, looking sad. Sydney skated over to her friend. "What's the matter, Kara?" she asked. "Aren't you having fun?"

"I'm scared to try to skate," Kara said. "I don't think I can do it."

Sydney had to decide. She could skate away and ignore Kara. She could say, "You're right. You probably can't skate." Or she could encourage Kara and say, "Yes, you can! I'll help you."

When someone said to Jesus, "I can't," He said, "Yes, you can if you have a little faith." Jesus encouraged people to have faith and trust God in everything they did. Faith can do amazing things. Faith helped David stand up to the giant, Goliath. Faith kept Shadrach, Meshach, and Abednego from getting burned in the fiery furnace. The Bible is filled with stories of faith! If you trust God to help you, He will give you courage to stand up to fear and try new things. It is good to encourage others. When you tell them, "Yes, you can," you are being like Jesus.

Sydney encouraged Kara to put on her skates and try. Can you guess what happened next? She helped Kara learn how to roller-skate—and Kara was soon having fun with all her friends.

In the **Spotlight**

Encourage: telling someone, "Yes, you can!"

Sparkling **SCRIPTURE**

*"So encourage each other and
build each other up."*

1 Thessalonians 5:11 nlt

Bright
IDEA

Make a tower! Use blocks, boxes,
pillows, or other light objects
that you can stack, and
see how high you can pile
them. Encouragement works
that way. Each little word of
encouragement is like a building
block. When you encourage people, you build them
up. You make them feel happy and tall.

Shine your LIGHT

Find one person this week who needs encouragement. It might be someone in your neighborhood, at school, or even in your own family. Say something that will build that person up:

"Great job!"

"You're awesome!"

"You deserve a hug!"

"Way to go!"

"Good try!"

Can you think of a few more ways to encourage others?

Polite and True

Some people don't know Jesus. If you talk about Him and about the Bible, they may not understand. Some kids might ask you why you believe in Jesus.

How you answer is important. The Bible says you should always be ready to answer anyone who asks you why you believe. So you need to have a plan. When someone asks, you can tell him that Jesus is your very best friend, He loves you, and He is with you all the time. You can also tell him about all the great things Jesus has done for you. You can even invite him to come with you to Bible class.

You should always be polite and respectful when answering your friends' questions about Jesus. If they don't want to listen, or even if they make fun of you, keep on being polite and respectful. That is what Jesus would do, and it's the right thing for you to do too.

Fill in the blanks to finish this sentence. You should always be _____ and _____ when answering your friends' questions about Jesus. Hint: you will find the answers in the devotion.

Shine your LIGHT

Make a list of all the things you can think of that Jesus has done for you. That will help you to be ready if your friends ask why you believe in Him. Practice with your family how you might answer a friend who asks you about Jesus.

God's Plan for You

*W*hat will you be when you grow up—a teacher, a parent, a doctor? You might know what you want to be, but God is the only one who knows what you *will* be.

God has a special plan for your life. He has known about it since before you were born, but He only shows it to you a little at a time. That's because God is in charge, and He doesn't want you running on ahead of Him, trying to make things happen. God likes to surprise you in wonderful little ways. He knows exactly how He is going to work out His plan for your future. He says His plan for you is good, and you shouldn't be afraid of not knowing what it is. You can trust Him never to do anything that will hurt you.

Your job is to keep God in your heart every day and shine His light on others. As you grow, God will show you more parts of His plan. He will put them into your heart at just the right time, and He will show you what to do.

God's plan for you will never end. Even after you die someday and go to live with Him in heaven, God has good things planned for you, great things that you can't begin to imagine. So don't worry about tomorrow. While you are busy living, God is busy working His plan for your future, and it's a wonderful plan, an amazing plan. Just you wait and see!

Sparkling **SCRIPTURE**

*"'I know what I have planned for you,'
says the Lord. 'I have good plans for you. . . .
I plan to give you hope and a good future.'"*

JEREMIAH 29:11

Bright IDEA

Draw a picture of what you want to be when you grow up. Then ask your mom or dad to put it in a safe place and keep it for you. Someday when you are all grown up, you can look at the picture again to see if your plan was the same as God's plan for you.

Shine your LIGHT

Get in the habit of listening for God in your quiet time with Him. God can speak quietly in your thoughts. Pay attention to the thoughts you have during your quiet time. Ask God to help you to hear and obey Him.

Celebrate!

*O*livia had a great time celebrating her birthday with her friends. She was happy playing with them all day long. But later in the day, Olivia felt grumpy. She didn't want to play, and she had a hard time getting along with her brothers. It felt like all the birthday happiness had drained out of her.

Olivia didn't like feeling unhappy, and she knew just what to do. She spent a little quiet time alone remembering that she is a child of God. That put a big smile on her face. Then she did her best to let her light shine by saying and doing kind things for others. Soon, Olivia's unhappiness turned into happiness, and she felt like celebrating again.

There is one kind of happiness that can never drain out of you—the happiness that comes from being a child of God. Your heavenly Father loves you so much, and when you keep

Him close to you, He can turn your unhappy heart into a happy one. God can fill you so full of joy that you'll want to sing, dance, and celebrate!

The next time you feel unhappy, do what Olivia did. Have a little quiet time with God, and celebrate that you are His amazing, wonderful, beautiful, one-of-a-kind child. Then do and say kind things, and feel your heart get happy again.

This game will make even the grumpiest person smile. Everyone sits in a circle. One person is "it." She has ten seconds to put on a big smile and try her best, without speaking, to get the other players to smile too. If other players smile, they are out of the game. After ten seconds, the girl who is "it" pretends to wipe the smile off her face and throw it to another person. Whoever lasts longest without smiling is the winner.

Sparkling **SCRIPTURE**

"Be full of joy in the Lord always."

PHILIPPIANS 4:4

Shine your LIGHT

Try to be happy every day. Happiness is something that you can spread around. When you are happy, people around you might catch your happiness and be happy too.

Our Now, Always, and Forever God

Yesterday, today, and forever—that's where God is. He is everything good, wonderful, and true. He made all the beautiful things you can think of, like colors, music, hugs, and wet puppy kisses. He made every living creature. He made the grass, flowers, fields, and oceans. And He keeps on making things!

God is with you wherever you go. He is with you when you are happy, sad, sick, and sleeping. God never changes. He doesn't get sick or take a break. He has the awesome power to be everywhere, all the time, at the same time, hearing you and helping you with whatever you need.

God made the sun to shine on you in the daytime and the stars and the moon to shine on you at night. God shines His light on you all the time. Best of all, He shines it brightly inside your heart. It is so big and bright that your heart can't hold it all.

God is love. His love spills out and into you. Then your light can shine brightly in God's wonderful world.

"Let it shine brightly," Jesus says. "Every day, let your light shine!"

Sparkling SCRIPTURE

"People don't hide a light under a bowl. They put the light on a lampstand. Then the light shines for all the people in the house. In the same way, you should be a light for other people. Live so that they will see the good things you do. Live so that they will praise your Father in heaven."

MATTHEW 5:15–16

Shine your LIGHT

Sing this song to remind you to let your light shine.

This Little Light of Mine

This little light of mine, I'm gonna let it shine.
This little light of mine, I'm gonna let it shine,
Let it shine, let it shine, let it shine.
All around the neighborhood, I'm gonna let it shine.
All around the neighborhood, I'm gonna let it shine,
Let it shine, let it shine, let it shine.
Let it shine till Jesus comes, I'm gonna let it shine.

Let it shine till Jesus comes. I'm gonna let it shine,
Let it shine, let it shine, let it shine.
Hide it under a bushel—NO! I'm gonna let it shine.
Hide it under a bushel—NO! I'm gonna let it shine,
Let it shine, let it shine, let it shine.
Let it shine in the whole wide world, I'm gonna let it shine.
Let it shine in the whole wide world, I'm gonna let it shine,
Let it shine, let it shine, let it shine.

Topical Index to Devotionals

The new **God's Little Angel**™ series

offers a comforting message for young readers
from bestselling author Sheila Walsh.

Gabby, God's Little Angel™

God loves you very much
and is always
watching over you!

Gabby's Stick-to-It Day

When it comes to doing
good, never give up!

*"He has put his angels in charge of you.
They will watch over you wherever you go."*

—PSALM 91:11